Built for Speed

The World's Fastest Trains

by Terri Sievert

Consultant:
Erik Sandblom
Regional Editor, Sweden and Norway
International Railway Journal
Editor, EriksRailNews.com

CAPSTONE
HIGH-INTEREST
BOOKS

an imprint of Capstone Press
Mankato, Minnesota

Capstone High-Interest Books are published by Capstone Press
151 Good Counsel Drive, P.O. Box 669, Mankato, Minnesota 56002
http://www.capstone-press.com

Library of Congress Cataloging-in-Publication Data

Sievert, Terri.
The world's fastest trains/by Terri Sievert.
    p. cm.—(Built for speed)
    Includes bibliographical references and index.
    Summary: Discusses the history and development of some of the world's
fastest trains.
    ISBN 0-7368-1061-7
    1. Express trains—Juvenile literature. [1. Express trains. 2. Railroads.]
I. Title. II. Built for speed (Mankato, Minn.)
TF573 .S56 2002
385'.2—dc21   2001003244

Editorial Credits
Angela Kaelberer, editor; Karen Risch, product planning editor; Timothy Halldin,
    cover designer and illustrator; Katy Kudela, photo researcher

Photo Credits
Archive Photos, 8
Bernard Boutrit/Woodfin Camp & Associates, Inc., 24
Beryl Goldberg, 20, 23, 38 (bottom), 39 (top)
Christian Charisius/Reuters/Archive Photos, 10, 30
Ernst Andreas Weigert, courtesy of Eisenbahn-Kurier, Germany, 29
HO/Reuters/Archive Photos, cover
Hulton/Archive Photos, 4, 6, 15
Koichi Kamoshida/Liaison Agency, 43
Michael Dalder/Reuters/Archive Photos, 26
Michael Smith/Liaison Agency, 32, 34, 37, 39 (bottom)
Mike Yamashita/Woodfin Camp and Associates, Inc., 40
Photo Network/Lonnie Duka, 12
Scott McDonald/Reuters/Archive Photos, 38 (top)
Susumu Takahashi/Reuters/Archive Photos, 16
Unicorn Stock Photos/Florent Flipper, 18

1 2 3 4 5 6 07 06 05 04 03 02

Table of Contents

Chapter 1

Rail History

In the 1500s, horses pulled the first railroad cars. The railroad cars carried metal ore from mines on rails made of wood.

The wooden rails wore down quickly. By the 1700s, people used iron rails and wheels. Each wheel had a flange to guide it along the track. This rim extends from the edge of the wheel. It keeps the wheel from slipping off the track.

Steam Trains

In 1804, Richard Trevithick invented the steam locomotive. It traveled 9 miles (14 kilometers) from Penydarren to the Glamorganshire Canal in southern Wales. The train pulled five wagons

Richard Trevithick invented the steam locomotive in 1804.

The streamliner Mallard set a speed record of
126 miles (203 kilometers) per hour.

and a passenger car. It carried 10 tons (9 metric
tons) of iron ore and 70 passengers. Its top
speed was 5 miles (8 kilometers) per hour.
Trevithick walked beside the train during its
first trip.

In 1825, workers finished building the first
passenger railroad. The track covered 25 miles
(40 kilometers) from Stockton to Darlington in
northeastern England. George Stephenson

designed the track's first train. It was called Locomotion. The train traveled 14 miles (23 kilometers) per hour.

In 1829, Stephenson built the Rocket. This train traveled 68 miles (109 kilometers) from Liverpool to Manchester, England. The Rocket completed the trip at a top speed of about 30 miles (48 kilometers) per hour.

Streamliners

Streamliners once were the fastest trains. They could travel more than 120 miles (193 kilometers) per hour. The British streamliner Mallard set a speed record when it traveled 126 miles (203 kilometers) per hour on July 3, 1938. A steam engine powered the Mallard. Its 1938 record still stands as the fastest speed for a steam engine.

The Mallard's shape was streamlined to make it cut through the air easily. Its design was based on a French race car. Its front end was curved. The train also had a double chimney to let out steam and smoke from the engine.

Today, visitors can see the Burlington Zephyr at the Museum of Science and Industry in Chicago.

Diesel-electric Trains

In 1892, German engineer Rudolf Diesel invented the diesel engine. Diesel engines compress air to produce heat. This heat then burns fuel.

By the 1920s, inventors used diesel engines to power trains. Diesel engines had several advantages over steam engines. Diesel engines used less fuel and needed fewer repairs than steam engines. Trains with diesel engines also could travel at higher speeds than trains with steam engines could. Most trains used diesel-electric engines. These diesel engines produce electric power that moves the wheels.

The U.S. train Burlington Zephyr was one of the first diesel-electric trains. This streamlined train set a distance record on May 26, 1934. The Zephyr traveled 1,015 miles (1,633 kilometers) from Chicago, Illinois, to Denver, Colorado. It completed this trip in 13 hours, 5 minutes.

World Speed Records

Electricity powers today's fastest trains. The French train Atlantique holds the electric train speed record. It set this record speed of 320 miles (515 kilometers) per hour on May 18, 1990.

Some trains use electricity and pieces of metal called magnets to float above the tracks. These trains are called maglev trains. The word "maglev" stands for "magnetic levitation." Objects that levitate float in the air.

People in Japan and other countries are testing maglev trains. On April 14, 1999, a maglev train set a new speed record. This train traveled 343 miles (552 kilometers) per hour on a test track in Japan.

HOW ELECTRIC TRAINS WORK

Electric trains run on electricity. An electric train does not carry its own fuel. A power plant produces electricity to power the train. The electricity travels to the train on wires. Electricity enters the train through a cable above the track. It also can enter the train on a third rail under the train.

Electrical cables hang from masts above the track. These masts sometimes are called pylons. A pantograph extends from the train's roof. This metal arm rubs against the cable to connect to the power source.

The electricity flows into a transformer inside the train. This device sends electricity to motors above the wheels. The motors are called traction motors. They make the wheels turn.

Chapter 2

Shinkansen

Japan was the first country to use high-speed trains. Japanese National Railways began building high-speed electric trains in 1959. Its bullet trains began operating in 1964.

Bullet trains were the first to provide passenger service at speeds of 100 miles (161 kilometers) per hour or faster. Today, Japan Railways Group operates the trains.

Bullet trains are named for their shape. The front end of a high-speed train is called the nose. The train's nose is pointed like a bullet.

The Japanese people call the bullet trains "Shinkansen." This word means "new trunk line." The early Shinkansen trains could travel as fast as 130 miles (209 kilometers) per hour.

Bullet trains are named for their shape.

Design

Bullet trains are designed to be aerodynamic. A bullet train's pointed nose and covered wheels help it cut quickly through the air. This design helps the train travel at high speeds.

Bullet trains also travel on straight, smooth tracks. These tracks have no sharp curves that would slow down the trains.

The bullet trains have an automatic safety system. This system stops the train if necessary. For example, objects may be on the track. The system can stop the train before it hits the objects.

Shinkansen Routes

Fast trains are important in Japan. This island nation's 126 million people live in a small area. This area is about the size of the U.S. state of Montana.

Tokyo is Japan's largest city. More than 8 million people live in the crowded city. High-speed trains allow people to live outside the city and travel quickly to work.

Japan's bullet trains began operating in 1964.

The first bullet train traveled from Tokyo to Osaka. This 320-mile (515-kilometer) route was called the New Tokaido Line. Today, bullet trains travel from Tokyo to Osaka in less than three hours.

Japan's four main islands have many mountains and valleys. The bullet train routes include many tunnels and bridges. The world's

longest tunnel is located in northern Japan. This tunnel is the Seikan tunnel. It is 33 miles (53 kilometers) long. It runs from Aomori on the island of Honshu to Hakodate on the island of Hokkaido. Nearly half of the tunnel is underwater.

Bullet Trains Today

In 1996, a test train set the record speed for bullet trains. This train reached a speed of 275 miles (443 kilometers) per hour. Bullet trains in regular service travel as fast as 186 miles (300 kilometers) per hour. Their average speed is 163 miles (262 kilometers) per hour.

Nearly 1 million passengers ride the bullet trains each day. The biggest trains have two levels and can carry 1,600 passengers. The longest trains have 16 cars. Passengers often work while they ride. Some of the newer trains have power outlets where people can plug in laptop computers.

The average speed of a bullet train is 163 miles (262 kilometers) per hour.

Chapter 3

TGV and Eurostar

France has been using high-speed trains since the 1970s. Its fast trains are called Train à Grande Vitesse (TGV). These words mean "high-speed train." The Société Nationale des Chemins de Fer Français (SNCF) operates the trains.

France's first high-speed trains had gas turbine engines. These engines compress air to burn fuel and turn it into pressurized gas. The gas spins a device called a turbine. The turbine is similar to a fan. It produces power as it spins.

Gas turbine engines weigh less than diesel engines. The lightweight engines allow trains to reach greater speeds. Trains with gas turbine

France's fast trains are called Train à Grande Vitesse (TGV).

The Paris Sud-Est was the first TGV train in service.

engines can travel faster than 150 miles (241 kilometers) per hour.

On December 8, 1972, a French train powered by a gas turbine engine reached a speed of 198 miles (318 kilometers) per hour. This speed set the record for a train with a gas turbine engine. This record still stands today.

The Paris Sud-Est and Atlantique

The SNCF also developed fast electric trains. The company tested the first electric TGV in 1978.

The first electric TGV system was called the Paris Sud-Est. The bright orange trains started scheduled service September 27, 1981. They traveled 317 miles (510 kilometers) between the cities of Paris and Lyon.

The TGV train Atlantique linked Paris and Bordeaux in 1990. The gray and blue train has a refreshment car and nine passenger cars. These cars can carry a total of 485 passengers.

On May 18, 1990, the Atlantique set the current electric train speed record. It reached a speed of 320 miles (515 kilometers) per hour.

Pantograph and Tracks

Electricity powers the TGV trains. Electricity enters the train through a pantograph. This metal arm is attached to the train's roof. The pantograph picks up electricity from overhead power lines. It sends the electricity into engines called locomotives at each end of the train.

The trains run fastest on special tracks. The tracks are used only for high-speed trains. They are smooth and straight. The tracks are expensive. The first TGV line cost $1.5 billion.

TGV Design
TGV trains have a streamlined design. A TGV train has a sloped nose to reduce air resistance. The trains are designed to be lightweight. The older TGV trains are made of steel. The newer trains are made of steel and lightweight metals such as aluminum and magnesium. The lightweight trains cause less damage to the tracks.

The train's wheels are between the train's cars. This placement makes the train more aerodynamic. It also makes it quieter than other trains.

Channel Tunnel
The Channel Tunnel links railroads in England and France. People often call it the Chunnel. The Chunnel runs under the English Channel. This body of water lies between England and France. The Chunnel runs 31 miles

TGV trains have a streamlined design.

(50 kilometers) from Folkstone, England, to near Calais, France.

Trains began running through the Chunnel in 1994. The trip takes about 20 minutes. The Chunnel has three underwater tunnels. The tunnels are 150 feet (46 meters) below the Channel floor. Two tunnels are for trains. The third tunnel is for repair and safety purposes.

Eurostar trains travel through the Chunnel between England and France.

The Eurostar

Today, electric Eurostar trains travel through the Chunnel from London, England, to Paris, France. Eurostar trains also travel to Brussels, Belgium. The largest Eurostar trains have 18 cars and can carry 766 passengers.

Three railway companies joined together to operate the Eurostar. These companies are

Eurostar in Great Britain, French Railways, and Belgian Railways.

The Eurostar's design is based on the French TGV train. The trains receive electricity from a pantograph on the roof or from a third rail on the ground.

Eurostar trains travel on high-speed lines in France and Belgium. They travel on standard railroad tracks in Great Britain. They reach speeds of 186 miles (300 kilometers) per hour on the high-speed tracks. They travel less than 100 miles (161 kilometers) per hour on standard tracks.

Cars and buses can travel through the Chunnel on an electric train called Le Shuttle. People can ride in the cars and buses as they travel through the Chunnel. Le Shuttle can carry as many as 120 cars, 12 buses, and 1,000 passengers. A Le Shuttle train leaves the station every 15 minutes.

Chapter 4

InterCity Express

The German National Railway Service oversees train service in Germany. This company is known as the Deutsche Bahn AG (DBAG).

Germany wanted to have trains that were as fast as France's TGV trains. In the 1980s, the DBAG developed the InterCity Express (ICE) trains. These electric trains began service in 1991.

Pantographs send electric power to the ICE train engines. Older ICE trains have two cars that provide power. One car is at the front of the train. The other is at the rear. Ten to 12 passenger cars are in between the two power cars. The newest ICE trains have a power supply in each car.

Pantographs send electric power to the ICE train engines.

Routes and Tracks

The ICE trains travel within Germany. They also travel from Germany to Switzerland, Austria, and the Netherlands.

The ICE travels on some new tracks. These straight tracks were built for the high-speed trains. The tracks are located between the cities of Hanover and Würzburg and between Mannheim and Stuttgart.

The ICE also travels on older tracks. The ICE trains only can run at their fastest speed on the new tracks. They must go at a slower speed on older tracks. The older tracks have more curves.

In May 1999, the DBAG began using a new ICE train on its route from Stuttgart, Germany, to Zurich, Switzerland. This train is called the ICE T.

The ICE T tilts inward as it speeds around curves. This ability allows it to travel 20 percent faster around curves than other ICE trains. A computer tells the ICE T how much to tilt around each curve.

The tilting technology of the ICE T is based on Italian trains called Pendolinos.

ICE trains such as this ICE 3 train travel within Germany and to several other countries in Europe.

These trains have been in service since 1987. Pendolinos travel 155 miles (250 kilometers) per hour on straight tracks. They use the tilting mechanism on curved tracks.

ICE Classes

The first ICE trains are called ICE 1 trains. In regular service, these trains have a top speed of 174 miles (280 kilometers) per hour. They can carry 645 people. In 1988, an ICE 1 train set a

On June 3, 1998, a serious train accident occurred at this site near Eschede, Germany.

speed record of 253 miles (407 kilometers) per hour. A TGV train broke this record the same year. The TGV train traveled 275 miles (443 kilometers) per hour.

In 1996, DBAG developed a new class of ICE trains. This class of trains is called ICE 2. The ICE 2 trains include one power car and seven passenger cars. Each train can carry 370 passengers.

The ICE 2 trains have several improvements over the original ICE trains. More seats can fit in each car with the same amount of room for passengers' legs. The trains have a restaurant car. They also have places for passengers to plug in portable computers.

DBAG introduced the newest class of ICE trains in 1999. The ICE 3 trains can travel 205 miles (330 kilometers) per hour. They can carry 415 passengers.

Safety

High-speed trains are very safe. Few crashes have occurred since the trains began operating in the 1960s.

A deadly high-speed train crash did occur on June 3, 1998. An ICE 1 train derailed near Eschede, Germany. The train then crashed into a concrete bridge. The crash killed 100 people and injured 88 others.

A broken tire on a wheel caused the crash. The wheel was not designed for high-speed trains. ICE trains now use steel wheels without tires.

Chapter 5

The Acela Express

Most high-speed trains are in Europe. But North American railway companies are beginning to develop high-speed trains.

The National Railroad Passenger Corporation oversees train service in the United States. This company is known as Amtrak. In the 1990s, Amtrak developed a high-speed electric train called the Acela Express. Amtrak now has 20 of these trains in service.

First Run
The first Acela Express went into service on November 16, 2000. It traveled between Washington, D.C., New York City, and Boston,

The high-speed Acela Express made its first run on November 16, 2000.

33

Massachusetts. This route is 457 miles
(735 kilometers) long.

In the past, Amtrak ran a standard train on
this route. This train was called the Metroliner.
The Acela Express can travel the 226 miles
(364 kilometers) between Washington and
New York in 2 hours, 44 minutes. It takes the
Metroliner 3 hours to make the same trip.
The Acela Express can travel the 231 miles
(372 kilometers) between New York and
Boston in 3 hours, 28 minutes. The Metroliner
takes 4 hours, 30 minutes on the same route.

Features

Two companies worked together to develop and
build the Acela Express. These companies are
Bombardier Transportation in Canada and
Alstom Limited in France. The train's design is
based on the TGV. The Acela Express also can
tilt around curves like the ICE T trains do.

In 1999, the Acela Express set a speed
record of 168 miles (270 kilometers) per hour
during a test run. In regular service, the train
has a top speed of 150 miles (241 kilometers)

**The Acela Express has a top speed of 150 miles
(241 kilometers) per hour.**

per hour. The train reaches this speed as it travels on 18 miles (29 kilometers) of straight track. This track is located in Rhode Island and Massachusetts. On other tracks, the train travels 135 miles (217 kilometers) per hour.

The Acela Express has a power car at the front and the rear. Five passenger cars and a dining car are between the power cars. The train can carry as many as 304 passengers.

The Acela Express has features that other U.S. passenger trains do not have. Its large seats have power outlets for laptop computers and headphones. In the dining car, passengers can watch videos on overhead screens. Passengers in first-class cars even can have their meals delivered to their seats. First-class passengers pay more money for their tickets than passengers in other classes.

Future of North American Trains

Amtrak hopes the Acela Express will interest North Americans in rail travel. The trains will operate first in the northeastern United States. Amtrak then may add more Acela Express routes in other areas of the United States. This expansion will be expensive. Amtrak will have

The control cab is located in the front power car of the Acela Express.

to straighten some curving tracks. It will have to improve and repair other tracks.

People in southern California are studying ways to bring high-speed rail travel to their area. Cities in southern California are crowded. Many of the people in these cities drive long distances to their jobs. Cars cause a great deal of pollution in these cities. High-speed trains may reduce this pollution.

FAST FACTS

SHINKANSEN

Operated By:	Japan Railways Group
First Used:	1964
Speed:	186 miles (300 kilometers) per hour
Record Speed:	275 miles (443 kilometers) per hour
Route:	Throughout Japan

TGV

Operated By:	SNCF
First Used:	1981
Speed:	186 miles (300 kilometers) per hour
Record Speed:	320 miles (515 kilometers) per hour
Route:	Throughout France and to England and Belgium

WORLD'S FASTEST TRAINS

INTERCITY EXPRESS

Operated By: DBAG
First Used: 1991
Speed: 205 miles (330 kilometers) per hour

Record
Speed: 253 miles (407 kilometers) per hour
Route: Throughout Germany and to Switzerland, Austria, and the Netherlands

ACELA EXPRESS

Operated By: Amtrak
First Used: 2000
Speed: 150 miles (241 kilometers) per hour

Record
Speed: 168 miles (270 kilometers) per hour
Route: Washington, D.C., to Boston, Massachusetts

Chapter 6

Future of
Fast Trains

Maglev trains use the power of magnets. These pieces of metal attract other metals.

The Earth has a magnetic force. The Earth's magnetic force is strongest at the North Pole and the South Pole. Each magnet has an end that is attracted to one of the poles. The unlike poles of two magnets attract each other. The like poles repel each other.

Maglev trains use powerful magnets with like poles under the train and on the guideway below. The poles push away from each other to hold the train about .4 inch (1 centimeter) in the air.

Electricity works with magnetic force to move the train forward. Electromagnets are attached to

Experimental maglev trains use the power of magnets to move forward.

the bottom of the train. These coils of metal wire are magnetized by electric currents. The tracks also have electromagnetic coils. A computer controls the magnets. The computer's commands hold the train in the air and move it forward.

Most trains produce friction as they travel over rails. This force slows down objects. But maglev trains ride on air. The lack of friction allows them to travel much faster than other trains.

Maglev History

German inventor Hermann Kemper developed magnetic train technology in the early 1920s. Since then, train companies in Europe, Asia, and the United States have tested maglev systems.

Maglev systems are expensive. Japan Railways spent $3 billion on 25 miles (40 kilometers) of test track west of Tokyo. Because of the cost, maglev trains may not be used for several years.

RUF

In 1988, Danish inventor Palle Jensen began work on a new kind of high-speed train system. The system is called Rapid, Urban, Flexible (RUF).

The RUF system combines a high-speed train with an electric car. Each adult in a city will

Japan Railways Group tests maglev trains on a test track near Tokyo.

have an electric car. People can use the car alone for short trips. The car will hook onto a high-speed train for longer trips. Jensen believes that the system will reduce traffic and pollution in large cities.

In June 2000, Jensen tested the RUF system on a test track in Denmark. The test was successful. But the system will need many more tests before passengers can use it.

Words to Know

aerodynamic (air-oh-dye-NAM-ik)—designed to move quickly and easily through the air

flange (FLANJ)—a rim on the edge of a wheel that keeps it on the tracks

friction (FRIK-shuhn)—a force created when two objects rub together; friction slows down objects.

levitate (LEV-i-tate)—to rise in the air and float

maglev (MAG-lev)—a train that moves above the track by the power of magnets; maglev is short for magnetic levitation.

pantograph (PAN-tuh-graf)—an arm that brings electricity from a power line to an electric train

turbine (TUR-buhn)—an engine powered by water, steam, or gas that moves through the blades of a fanlike device and makes it turn

To Learn More

Biello, David. *Bullet Trains: Inside and Out.* Technology—Blueprints of the Future. New York: PowerKids Press, 2002.

Cefrey, Holly. *High Speed Trains.* Built for Speed. New York: Children's Press, 2001.

Chant, Christopher. *High-Speed Trains.* The World's Railroads. Philadelphia: Chelsea House Publishers, 2000.

Useful Addresses

Amtrak
30th Street Station
Fifth Floor South
Philadelphia, PA 19104

Deutsche Bahn AG
BestellCenter Elektronische Medien
Postfach 1157
53821 Troisdorf
Germany

Japan Railways Group—New York Office
One Rockefeller Plaza
Suite 1622
New York, NY 10020

Internet Sites

Amtrak
http://www.amtrak.com

Die Bahn—InterCity Express
http://www.bahn.de/pv/int_guest/true/
    pv2_trains_ice.shtml

European Railway Server
http://mercurio.iet.unipi.it

**How Stuff Works—How Maglev Trains
   Will Work**
http://www.howstuffworks.com/maglev-train.htm

International Railway Journal
http://www.railjournal.com

SNCF.com
http://www.sncf.com/indexe.htm

Index